Psst...

Secret Instructions Every Girl Should Know

by
Rick Walton
and
Cheri Earl

★ American Girl®

Published by American Girl Publishing, Inc.

Copyright © 2009 by American Girl, LLC

Questions or comments? Call 1-800-845-0005,
visit our Web site at **americangirl.com**,
or write to Customer Service, American Girl, 8400 Fairway Place, Middleton, WI 53562-0497.

Printed in China
09 10 11 12 13 14 15 16 LEO 10 9 8 7 6 5 4 3 2 1

All American Girl marks are trademarks of American Girl, LLC.

Editorial Development: Trula Magruder

Art Direction & Design: Chris Lorette David

Production: Jeannette Bailey, Julie Kimmell, Sarah Boecher, Judith Lary, Sally Wood

Photography
Cover, Secret 15, and Secret 87: Steven Talley, Art Direction by Julie Mierkiewicz
Secret 33: Jim Jordan, Art Direction by Julie Mierkiewicz
Secrets 44 and 48: Jim Jordan
Secret 79: Thomas Heinser, Art Direction: Julie Mierkiewicz

Dear Reader,

Want to know a secret? We all have secrets! We love those little bits of information that very few people know. Secrets remind us that there's mystery in the world.

Inside, you'll discover 90 secrets. Some you may have heard. Some may surprise you. But most will help you to better understand the world around you.

The best thing about *these* secrets is that you can tell them. Whisper them to your friends. Share them with your sister. Mention a few to your mom.

And then after reading all the secrets inside this book, go on a search for even more secrets. Unravel life's little mysteries—one secret at a time.

Your friends at American Girl

Contents

Secret #1

Keeping a Secret

Do you want to know the easiest way to keep a secret? DON'T TELL ANYONE. If you don't tell, the secret won't get out. Don't say, "I'll just tell this one person." If you do, the person you tell might tell one person, and that person might tell another person, and so on. Keeping a secret means keeping silent.

Secret #2

Seeking a Celebrity's
Photo or Autograph

To contact a celebrity, write to her official fan club, her manager, the team she plays for, the studio that produces her TV show or movies, her music company—whatever organization she works with. Then tell her what you're looking for. If it's a photo, send a stamped envelope that's big enough for the picture. If it's an autograph, send a photo or card to sign. Finally, cross your fingers and wait.

Best
Wishes,
Jen!
Love,

Secret #3

Telling the Temperature by Listening to Insects

Want to know the temperature outside without a thermometer? Listen to the bugs.

Cricket chirps:

1. Count the number of chirps in 15 seconds.

2. Add 37. Your final number is the temperature in Fahrenheit.

This is a cricket.

Katydid chirps:

1. Count the number of chirps in a minute.

2. Subtract 19.

3. Divide by 3.

4. Add 60. Your final number is the temperature in Fahrenheit.

This is a katydid.

MY FORT BLUEPRINT

grass roof

door

window

welcome

Building an Outdoor Fort from a Box

Turn a giant box upside down. Boxes that hold refrigerators, washers, or dryers work best. Ask an adult to help cut out windows and a door. Disguise the fort with hay, brush, leaves, or grass clippings.

Secret #5

Landing on a Game Show

Before auditioning, practice, practice, practice. Play along with the game on TV. Study the categories of questions. Analyze the show's winners. And if available, play the board-game or computer-game versions until you feel prepared. Then follow the show's audition instructions to the letter (available on the TV show or the show's Web site). If you land an audition, be professional and positive, but have fun. Producers love interesting contestants. And if you make it on the show, enjoy the experience—whether you win all that cash or not.

Secret #6

Attracting Butterflies

Design a butterfly rest area. Plant colorful, fragrant flowers where there's lots of sun and little wind. Make small puddles so the butterflies can drink. Add flat stones so they can rest. And toss out rotting fruit so they can eat. If all this fails, visit a butterfly farm and bring some home!

Blowing a Double Bubble

Chew two pieces of soft bubble gum until they're flavorless. Press the gum against the back of your front teeth with your tongue. Push your tongue forward into the gum to make an air pocket. Blow slowly and evenly to stretch out the gum. Press your lips together to seal the bubble. Gather the leftover gum in your mouth and get ready to make another bubble. Push your tongue inside the bubble you've already blown. Slowly blow a smaller bubble. Press your lips to seal again. Double bubble!

Secret #8

Removing Chewing Gum from Your Hair

Gum loves oil and fat even more than it loves your hair. So if a big bubble lands in your locks, put down the scissors and rub oil on the gum—baby oil, oily lotion, even cooking oil. Then rub in conditioner until you see the gum start to break down. Next, strip away the pieces with a paper towel and run a fine-toothed comb through your hair. Finally, wash out the oil and conditioner with warm water.

Secret #9

Preparing for School

On the night before school, choose what you'll wear and lay it out—everything from underwear to jewelry. Pack your bus pass, homework, and anything else you'll need. Put the pack by the door. Add a coat, hat, and umbrella if you'll need them. Make breakfast and stick it in the fridge: peanut butter on a bagel, fresh fruit and yogurt, a breakfast bar, or leftover pizza. Will you want a shower? Take it now.

take me

Secret #10

Getting Ready for School in 11 Minutes

You'll get a few more minutes of sleep with this schedule, but it works only if you've prepared the day before. (See "Preparing for School" on the left page.)

1. Get up, go to the bathroom, and wash. (2 minutes)

2. Brush your teeth. (2 minutes)

3. Dress and brush your hair. (2 minutes & 30 seconds)

4. Eat breakfast. (4 minutes)

5. Grab your coat and backpack and go! (30 seconds)

Secret #11

Avoiding a Yawn

You can't always avoid yawning, but you can try. To start, think about something else. Then take deep breaths. Next, swallow a lot. Even after all that, you might still feel like yawning.

Secret #12

Making Someone Yawn

The next time you're talking to friends, tell a story about a pal who couldn't quit yawning. Then describe how you yawned. Be cool—don't give it away that you're trying to get your friends to yawn. Try not to yawn yourself . . . if you can. After someone yawns, let everyone in on your experiment.

Secret #13

Teaching Your Dog to Shake

Have your dog sit in front of you. Show it a treat, and then gently take a paw in your hand as you say "Shake." Give the dog the treat while its paw is still in your hand. Practice every day, and give your dog lots of praise.

Secret #14

Scooping Ice Cream

Run a spoon or an ice-cream scoop under hot water, and then quickly scoop the ice cream with it. The heated spoon will melt its way right through your frozen treat.

Secret #15

Being Liked Right Away

To make a new friend, follow five steps:

1. **Smile.** Others will see you as friendly and easy to talk to.

2. **Chat.** Say something nice, but put some thought into your compliment, such as, "I loved the answer you gave in class."

3. **Listen.** Pay attention to what the person says and comment on it. Don't talk only about your interests.

4. **Chip in.** Contribute to the discussion and ask questions. If your new friend asks a question, think about how you really feel and tell her. Don't just shrug and stare.

5. **Care.** Be a good friend. Don't gossip or say hurtful things. People like to be around sincerely nice friends.

Secret #16

Estimating Your Kitten's Age

Weigh your kitten. Add one month for each pound. So if the cat weighs 3 pounds, most likely it's three months old. This works only up to 4½ pounds.

Secret #17

Calculating Your Cat's Age in Human Years

At one year, the cat is 15 human years old. At two years, it's 24 years old. For each additional year, add four human years.

Secret #18

Calculating Your Dog's Age in Human Years

At one year, the dog is 15 human years old. At two years, it's 24 years old. For each additional year, add four human years.

Secret #19

Calculating Your Horse's Age in Human Years

At one year, the horse is 6½ human years old. At two years, it's 13 years old. At three years, it's 19½ years old. For each additional year, add 2½ human years.

Secret #26

Estimating Your Parrot's Age in Human Years

At four years, the parrot is 15 human years old. For each additional year, add one human year.

Secret #21

Estimating Your Guinea Pig's Age in Human Years

At six weeks, the guinea pig is 15 human years old. For each additional *month*, add one human year.

Inventing a New Recipe

Chefs invent new recipes every day. So can you.

1. Combine foods that aren't usually served together—cheese and jam, or peanut butter and banana on a tortilla.

2. Prepare (fry, freeze, bake, blend, or spice) a food in a way it's not normally made—freeze grapes or carbonate yogurt.

3. Change ingredients in or instructions for a recipe—instead of a sausage and cheese pizza, use jam and fruit for a dessert pizza.

Now taste it. If your new recipe tastes great, share it!

Being Alone but Not Lonely

Nobody can be a better friend to you than you. So spend time alone. Write a fan letter. Read a book. Make a meal for your family. Organize your room. Write a song. Practice handstands. Or sit and think. Get to know yourself better.

secret #24

Blowing Out Birthday Candles

Get ready: Make sure your hair's up or out of the way. Now, position your head so that you're facing down, about a foot above the center of the cake.

Get set: Take a deep breath.

Blow: Force all the air out of your lungs in one quick, giant burst. Aim right for the center of the cake. Happy birthday!

Secret #25

Naming Your Racehorse

Think this is easy? If you register your racehorse, you'll have lots of naming rules. For instance, you can't name the horse after someone living unless that person gives permission. Your horse can't have the same name as any other racehorse in the country. And you can use only 18 letters in the name—including spaces. You could follow tradition and create a name that refers to each parent. For example, if the dad is named *Thunderbolt* and the mom is called *Take a Hike,* you could name your horse *Storm Walker.* See? Or, don't register your racehorse. Then you can name it anything you like!

Secret #26

Speaking Pig Latin

For words that begin with consonants, move the first letter or cluster of letters to the end of the word and add "ay."

three = eethray   please = easeplay   pig = igpay

For words that begin with vowels, just add "ay" or "way" to the end.

a = way   eagle = eagleway   it = itay   arm = armay

Split compound words into two words.

bedroom = edbay oomray

toothbrush = oothtay ushbray

wallpaper = allway aperpay

Ownay ivegay itay ayay rytay ouryay elfsay!

Secret #27

Teaching Your Dog to Roll Over

Get your dog to lie down. Say "Roll" as you slowly bring a treat over her shoulders in the direction you'd like her to roll. At the beginning, help her roll with a gentle push. After she finishes a roll, give her a treat. Keep practicing! When she finally gets it, reward her with hugs and praise, instead of a treat each time.

Secret #28

Packing for a Slumber Party

In an overnight bag, pack a sleeping buddy—a stuffed animal or a hug pillow. Drop in hair accessories to try out salon styles. Bring a few DVDs for movie fun. Carry a game for after-movie madness. Slip in CDs for dancing. Add a flashlight to find late-night snacks. Grab a camera for party-pic memories. Roll pj's, clothes, a toothbrush, and a pillow inside your sleeping bag. You're ready!

Secret #29

Writing a Joke

One way to invent a new joke is to follow the "Change the Famous Name" formula. It goes like this:

1. Choose a famous name, such as Cinderella.

2. Look at Cinderella's name. How could you change it? How about "Cinderelephant"? This is your punch line.

3. List two things that make up the punch line. In this case, they're "Cinderella" and "elephant."

4. Write a question that suggests the two things in your punch line without naming them: "Who had big ears, weighed 7,000 pounds, and married a handsome prince?"

5. Put your question and punch line together: "Who had big ears, weighed 7,000 pounds, and married a handsome prince? Cinderelephant!"

Now try one on your own.

Stopping a Brain Freeze

A brain freeze lasts only one to five minutes, and it's not dangerous. But if you hate the pain, try this: Quickly warm your palate. Eat or drink something warm or press your tongue against the roof of your mouth. The best solution is to prevent the freeze from happening in the first place. Eat a frozen treat s-l-o-w-l-y. If you feel a brain freeze coming on, take a break from your cold food until the roof of your mouth warms up, and then start eating again.

Secret #31

Winning a Class or School Election

Show schoolmates that you really care. Get involved in school activities. Be friendly. Ask students what they want changed. Don't attack your opponents, but focus on the positive things *you'll* do. Make realistic campaign promises. Then talk to the students again. Really listen, and you'll earn their trust.

Vote for Cara!

Secret #32

Dealing with a Bad Gift

No gift is worth ruining a friendship over. If you receive a horrible present from a friend, be tactful. Find one thing you like about the gift and offer a sincere thanks: "Oh, purple is my favorite color!" If you can't think of anything, thank the friend. But don't *overdo* thanking her, or you won't sound sincere.

Secret #33

Diving into a Pool

If you can swim and diving is allowed at your pool, stand at the side of the deep end, with one foot slightly behind the other. Line up the big toe of your front foot with the edge of the pool. Hold your arms out in front of you and look down at the bottom of the pool. Slowly fall into the pool headfirst. As you practice, gently push off from the side of the pool as you dive. Eventually, you'll dive out a bit instead of straight down. Be sure to practice when there's a lifeguard or parent present.

Secret #34

Teaching Your Dog to Turn Around

1. Have your dog stand facing you. Show her a treat in your hand.

2. Say, "Turn around."

3. Now hold the treat in front of her nose and lead her around so she walks in a circle. Don't let her get the treat—yet.

4. After she makes the circle and she's facing you, say, "Good dog!" and give her the treat.

5. Repeat for only a few minutes everyday. Remember, you don't want her to get bored!

Secret #35

Finding a Friend When You're the New Girl

Throw a getting-to-know-me party. Form a study group. Take an after-school class that interests you. Eat lunch in the cafeteria and meet girls from other homerooms. Volunteer at an animal shelter or nursing home. Join a club. Visit the library. Just get out there and smile!

Secret #36

Using Feng Shui in Your Room

To increase the good vibes in your room, remove or hide electronics—they zap positive energy. Position your bed so that you can see the door, but don't put it next to a window or a noisy wall. Try blue or green bedsheets to calm you. Add a live plant to symbolize growth, life, and well-being. The Chinese use bamboo. They think it's a symbol of good luck, and it grows really fast.

Secret #37

Receiving a Reply from a Favorite Author

Most authors will write back if they think you've put thought into your letter. So if you're writing on an author's Web site, read all the questions submitted to her Web page, and then write a question she hasn't answered. If you're writing a letter, ask a question that shows you've paid close attention to a specific book or that reveals you are a true fan.

Secret #38

Attracting Birds to a Birdbath

Fill a birdbath with 2½ inches of water. If you add more water, birds will be afraid of the bath. If you add less, it'll be tougher for them to bathe. Keep the bath sparkling clean—you wouldn't want a dirty swimming pool, either.

Secret #39

Making Vacuuming Fun

Start well into a room and then tell yourself that once you've vacuumed a spot, you can't step on it again. Work your way out of the room. Play music. Promise yourself a treat as soon as you finish the job.

Secret #40

Taking Fingerprints

Clean each fingertip with alcohol and wipe it dry. Roll the fingertip from one side of the nail to the other on a black ink pad, and then roll it in the same way on a white card or piece of paper. Repeat with each finger. Clean your fingers again with alcohol to remove the ink. If you'd like to compare fingerprints, ask a family member or friend if you can take her prints, too.

Secret #41

Reading Fingerprints

Take an impression of each finger (see the page at left), and then examine your prints on the paper with a magnifying glass. See how each fingertip has a repeating pattern of loops, whorls, or arches? Compare your fingerprints with a friend's or sibling's prints. Even if you both have the same pattern, you'll see differences such as wide spaces or broken lines. No one has prints exactly like yours—not even a twin.

Arch Pattern
Ridges enter from one side of your finger, make a mountain-like shape in the middle, and then go out the opposite side.

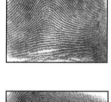

Loop Pattern
Ridges enter from both sides, curve in the middle, loop back around, and go out the same side they came in.

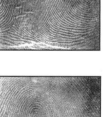

Whorl Pattern
Ridges make a big whirlpool circle in the middle of your finger.

Secret #42

Making Friends Laugh

Making people laugh takes more planning than wearing a clown suit and a red squeaky nose to class (although that's pretty funny). If none of the following tips work, laugh a lot anyway. Laughing is contagious, you know!

Pay attention to the details most people miss.

> Why do we call blackboards black? Aren't most of them green?

Mimic or imitate the sounds and movements of real things.

> Rrr-rrr-rrr-rrr. We really need a new pencil sharpener.

Keep jokes and stories short, or you'll give your audience time to get bored or distracted.

> Is it weird in here, or is it just me?

Make fun of yourself. Making fun of others isn't funny.

> I would love to get to the point, if I could only reach it.

Secret #43

Guessing the Length of Shoelaces

Tell a friend wearing laces that you can pretty much guess how long her shoelaces are in inches. How do you do it? Count the number of eyelets in her shoe and multiply by two. Voilà! Pull out a ruler if she wants to remove her laces to confirm.

Secret #44

Keeping a Ponytail Holder in Thin or Slick Hair

A sliding ponytail holder can drive you crazy. Spritz your hair with water before you pull it back. This will give your ponytail holder much more grip.

Secret #45

Preventing Carpet Shock

Don't walk around on carpeting in your socks—and avoid
touching anything metal, such as a doorknob. If you must
open a door, touch the knob first with a key or a coin. The
shock will go into the metal before it goes into you. Or use
your arm to touch the door. Your arm won't feel the shock as
strongly as a finger.

Secret #46

Eating with Chopsticks

Don't be afraid of the sticks—they make eating so much fun!

1. Lay the thick end of the first chopstick between your thumb and index finger. Let the chopstick rest against your middle fingertip.

2. Hold the second chopstick between the tips of your thumb and index finger. The first chopstick stays still. Move the second chopstick up and down.

Practice picking up small bits of food. Then try pinching clumps of rice.

Secret #47

Telling If a Friend Is Lying

Telling the difference between a truth and a lie isn't easy.

Someone who is lying may repeat your questions back to you.

> Did you forget my party?

> Did I forget your party?

Or she may act as if she can't remember things she should be able to remember.

> Why didn't you show up at the library on Saturday?

> I think I did show up. I can't remember.

She may make strong promises or pledges.

> My sister saw you at the movies with Jenny.

> I was not at the movies with Jenny. Cross my heart and hope to die!

Or she may name someone who can testify that she's honest.

> I think you're lying to me.

> I am not lying—you can ask my mom!

Notice body language. If she fidgets, crosses her arms, or covers her mouth to answer a question, she might be lying. On the other hand, she might just be shy. So watch and listen carefully, and you'll figure out whether or not she's telling the truth.

Secret #48

Making the Perfect Hair Part

Use the pointed end of a tail comb to create all kinds of hair parts—from a straight one to a zigzag. Hold the comb end at a 45-degree angle and keep it in constant contact with your scalp while drawing the part you like.

Secret #49

Remembering Information for a Test

You'll have a greater chance of acing an exam if you relax and try to make the information funny. Say you need to remember that penguins live in Antarctica. Imagine those funny birds camping out in your aunt's house—Aunt Arctica. Study your information in small chunks, and take a short break between chunks. Finally, repeat your facts every day for a week. Most likely, you won't forget a thing.

Secret #50

Remembering a Name

Use that person's name a lot during your conversation. If it's an unusual name, ask her how she spells it. Then connect her name to something that will remind you of her: "Madison acts like my cousin who lives in Madison!" After she leaves, write down her name and a few notes about her. Look at your notes from time to time. The next time you see Madison, her name will pop into your head. And if not, say, "Hi, I'm Erin. What is your name again?"

Secret #51

Preventing Split Ends

The only way to get rid of split ends is to ask a stylist or adult to snip them off. To prevent more split ends, using conditioner on the ends of your hair after shampooing will keep them from drying out.

Secret #52

Inviting Guests to a Party

Your party begins with an invitation. You're offering guests a hint of what's to come. Mail or e-mail your invitations to guests—especially if the number of guests you can invite is limited. In the invitation, explain the party theme and any special instructions on what to wear or bring. List the party's start and end times, a phone number so that guests can R.S.V.P. (please respond), and directions or a map to your party. Send the invitations three weeks in advance.

Come to a Pajama Jam!

Where Emily's house

925 Cloud Nine Lane

When Friday, May 3

5:00 P.M. to 10:00 A.M.

Special Instructions Bring a sleeping bag and pillow. My mom will bring you home on Saturday morning.

RSVP 555-8372

It's a Pa

Secret #53

Being a Great Party Hostess

Want to be a great hostess? Be yourself and make sure your guests feel welcome and included. It's also your job to make sure guests aren't hungry, thirsty, or bored. And if something goes wrong with a snack or game, laugh it off or make a joke about it to keep your guests comfortable.

Blowing Up a Balloon

Skip blowing up a balloon with your mouth—it can cause you to feel light-headed. Balloon pumps are inexpensive and save you from the danger of a balloon popping in your face. To start, roll the balloon end over the pump nozzle. Hold the balloon end, the nozzle, and the pump in one hand while you work the handle with the other. Don't overfill or the balloon will pop. Pinch the balloon closed, pull it off the nozzle, and tie it.

Tying Off a Balloon

If the balloon is overinflated, let out enough air so that you can stretch the balloon neck around two fingers. Next, roll the end through the loop, making a knot. Pull your fingers out of the loop, and then stretch the knot gently to tighten it.

Deflating a Balloon

Try this ear-friendly method to deflate balloons. Hold the balloon just above the knot and pinch the neck closed. Snip off the knot with scissors, and then slowly let the air escape.

Secret #57

Getting a Toddler to Do What You Want Her to Do

Give a toddler two choices that lead to the same result. "Annie, do you want to eat the scrambled egg with a fork or with your fingers?" Either way she chooses, Annie's eating her breakfast.

Secret #58

Attracting Hummingbirds

To attract hummingbirds, plant sweet, red, tubular flowers. Make a drink from one part sugar and four parts water. Fill a red feeder with the drink and hang it over the flowers. Just when you think it's not working, you might see a teeny-tiny bird buzzing around those blooms.

Secret #59

Making a Birthday Cake
Look Extra Special

A beautiful birthday cake can get lost on a table filled with foods, drinks, and party decorations. To make it stand out, lift it up! Drape a tablecloth over a phone book or a shoebox. Now display your special cake on the raised platform.

Secret #60

Adding Numbers Instantly

Adding 100 Numbers

Tell a friend that you can add 100 numbers in a couple of seconds. Ask her to choose any number that ends in two zeros. Suppose she chooses 1,200. Announce that the sum of all her numbers from 1,200 to 1,299 (that's 100 numbers total) equals 124,950.

How do you do it?

Take the numbers that come before the two zeros—in this case, 12—and always tack the numbers 49 and 50 onto the end in that order—so you'll get 124,950. If the friend challenges you, hand her a calculator and say, "Start adding."

Adding 1,000 Numbers

You can add 1,000 numbers using the same method. Just ask the friend to choose a number that ends in three zeroes, and instead of tacking on 49 and 50, tack on 499 and 500 to the end.

Secret #61

Telling a Real Pearl from a Fake One

The most valuable pearls are natural ones that grow in oysters without any human help. Cultured pearls are natural, too, but pearl farmers helped these along by planting a bead inside the oyster to get the process started. If pearls don't come from an oyster, they're fake—made of plastic, glass, or some other material. Real pearls aren't perfect. Hold a magnifying glass up to a strand of pearls. Do you see ridges, irregularities, and different sizes and shapes? If so, they're probably real. Look at the hole. Do you see layers peeling off? If so, they're probably artificial. Cultured pearls occasionally flake, but natural pearls never do.

Secret #62

Making Dozens of Pancake-Syrup Flavors

With an adult's help, you can create a variety of flavorful syrups for pancakes, waffles, or French toast.

1. Ask an adult to bring 1 cup of water to a low boil.

2. Add 2 cups of sugar, and stir until the sugar dissolves.

3. Stir in 1 package of a powdered drink mix in a favorite flavor.

4. Stir until the syrup thickens, and then let it cool before using. Repeat with other drink-mix flavors.

Secret #62

Creating Invisible Ink

Send a friend a message that no one else can see. Pour a little lemon juice into a glass, soak a cotton swab in the juice, and write a message on paper. Pass the paper to a friend who knows to warm it under a light until the message appears.

Secret #64

Making Your Own Soda Pop

Combine ½ cup fruit juice without pulp with ½ cup sparkling water. Add ice if you'd like. Eureka! Soda pop.

Secret #65

Chitchatting with Your Cat

Your cat understands when you're praising, scolding, or just talking with her by the tone of your voice. She understands words that are important to her, such as "treat" or "go outside." So the more you talk to your cat, the more she'll talk to you. Here's what she might already be saying:

If your cat is purring, notice her ears. If they're up and alert, she's relaxed. If they're back flat, she's nervous or scared.

I'm fine, really.

The "ow" sound a cat makes, like "meOW" or "wOw," might mean that she wants to go outside, she wants you to open a door, or she likes the sound of her voice in an open area.

Are you listening?

The high-pitched, loud sound your cat makes when she growls or screams with her mouth open means that she's upset. You've likely heard this when another cat came around.

I'm angry!

Secret #66

Sleeping When
You're
Afraid of the Dark

If the night spooks you, try these bright ideas: Plug in a night-light. Listen to a favorite, upbeat CD. Share a room with a sister. Read a funny book. Decorate your room with things that make you happy and comfortable. Leave your door open. Feel better?

Secret #67

Keeping Soda Pop from Bubbling Out of Your Glass

Tilt your glass at a slight angle and slowly pour the soda. Make sure that the soda touches only the side of your glass. Don't let it pour into the soda already in your glass. You can also pour the soda over a spoon or another clean object and avoid foam.

stop quaddling!

secret #68

Making a Word Trendy

Want to make a word trendy in your school? Get others to use that word until it catches on. For instance, if you like the word quaddle (which means "to grumble or complain"), call people quaddlers instead of whiners. Ask friends to stop quaddling. Be committed, and you'll start hearing your word in the halls.

Secret #69

Changing Your Name

The easiest way to change your name is to pick a new name and use it. This is called "common usage." Family and friends may prefer your new name if it's a version of your old name or it's a middle name. The other way to change your name requires your parents to fill out a lot of paperwork, file a petition, and bring you to a state court. So common usage is your best option.

Just call me Nicky.

Secret #70

Requesting a Song on the Radio

Find the phone number to the station you like, and call. If the phone is busy, keep calling. When someone answers, tell her what you want her to play. Be ready to say your first name and to shout out the station's name, if she asks. Then listen for your song. It might take a while, so be patient.

WMAG plays the biggest hits!

Secret #71

Not Being Afraid When a Friend Tells a Ghost Story

If ghost stories scare you, don't listen to them. You can tell the person about to recite the tale that you don't want to hear it, or you can try these ghost busters.

Think like a scientist.

Analyze the story as it's told and you'll find reasons why it can't be true.

Make the scary story disappear.

Hum a tune in your head while thinking of a cute puppy. Or add silly things to the story—give the ghost a tutu and fill the haunted house with bunnies.

Don't think about the story when it's over.

Talk about something that makes you feel happy or do an activity with the lights on.

Secret #72

Finding a Lost Pet's Owner

If a stray pet finds you, ask a parent to help you bring it to a local animal shelter. The owner has a better chance of finding her pet there. Ask the shelter how long the owner has to claim the pet, and then check back on that day. If the owner never claims it, then you and your family can decide whether or not to adopt the pet.

Secret #73

Finding Your Lost Pet

If you lose a pet, go with a parent to check animal shelters every day (don't just call). Talk to people who live near where you lost your pet. Put up flyers around the neighborhood that show your pet's photo or hang flyers where people with pets go, such as veterinarians' offices, grocery stores, pet groomers, and so on. Put an ad in all the area newspapers. Contact animal shelters within 20 miles of where you lost the animal. Use your parent's name and phone number as the contact.

Lost Cat!

Sweet and friendly cat answers to the name of Callie. Please call 555-7842

secret #74

Standing Out in Your
Teacher's Eyes

Join in class discussions, but don't take over. Put a lot of thought into your homework. Your teacher will appreciate your insights and will remember you as a student who cares. Be kind and helpful to the other kids in class, especially those who are having trouble or who aren't popular. If you have a question—especially if you're struggling with a subject—stay after class and talk to the teacher about it. That way, when it comes time to do grading, your teacher won't think you're making mistakes because you don't care.

Secret #75

Finding Your Personal Style

Find a style that screams, "This is ME!" Then keep wearing it. Don't wear something that you think looks weird just to be different. Ask family and friends what they think. Before long you'll have created a signature look. And that's a good thing.

Choosing a Room Color You'll Love

When you're choosing outfits, looking at a box of crayons, or flipping through magazines, is there a color that always makes you happy? With a parent's help, find a sample of this color and take it to the paint store. Choose a paint that's a bit lighter than the color you like, because the larger the area, the darker the color will look. Buy a quart of paint and paint two or three coats on a large piece of white cardboard. Let it dry for 24 hours. Now, lie on your bed and look at the board. Do you like how the color makes you feel? Do you like how the color goes with the furnishings? Do you like the color when the sun hits it and when the room gets darker? If so, you're set to buy more paint. If not, try again. It's only paint!

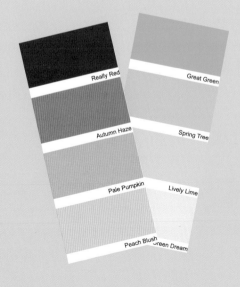

Really Red

Great Green

Autumn Haze

Spring Tree

Pale Pumpkin

Lively Lime

Peach Blush

Green Dream

Secret #77

Winning a Writing Contest

Begin your next writing contest with a brainstorm. Let's say an essay topic is titled "Whoops!" Think of things you've accidentally done or said. Make a list of these experiences. Look over your list, and choose the funniest, most exciting, or saddest idea. When you write the essay, fill it with interesting details—judges choose stories that hold their attention. Ask a teacher or a family member to read your essay. Take notes of her suggestions and make revisions. Send the essay in on time. Then wait around until you hear from the judges—or enter another contest!

Secret #78

Winning at Tic-Tac-Toe

You'll have a good chance of winning at Tic-Tac-Toe if you're X and you get to go first. And you'll increase that chance if you place that X in a corner or the center square. O will be forced to block your move each time to keep from losing, and that can get discouraging for O. But if you end up being O, don't get discouraged or you'll risk missing the best place to block your opponent. If neither of you makes a mistake, the game will always end in a tie—and that's not losing!

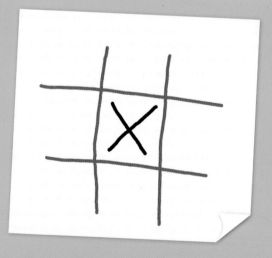

Teaching a Dog Any Trick

Make learning fun, and your dog will do anything to please you. Give treat rewards and lots of praise. But don't practice a trick for more than a few minutes at a time, or you'll bore your dog. And be patient. Some dogs learn faster than others. You may have to repeat a trick many times for days or even weeks before she gets it. Always treat your pet with kindness.

Secret #80

Keeping a Campout Stress-Free

Pack anything that will make you feel cozy in your tent. Bring comfortable warm clothes, well-made sleeping gear, and books or puzzles. Get ready for bed while it's still light outside. As soon as the sun sets, keep a flashlight nearby to shine light on anything that might startle you. Listen to a personal music player as you fall asleep.

Secret #81

Getting Paid to Babysit

Before you accept the job, discuss with the parents the amount you charge to babysit. Then they'll know that you expect to be paid. At the same time, be aware of their expectations. If a parent wants you to put the kids to bed, and you don't do that, they might not want to pay you what was negotiated—or they'll pay you, but won't want to hire you again next time.

Secret #82

Winning a Dog Show

Register your purebred dog with the American Kennel Club, and then join your local kennel club. Train your dog. If your dog's not well-trained and well-behaved, she'll never win. Attend classes with your dog to practice for a show. Train yourself, too. Learn command forms used at dog shows, and know how to groom and present your dog. Go to the AKC Web site, and download judging sheets to see what judges expect. Attend shows. Watch videos of previous shows. Notice what sets winning owners and winning dogs apart from other participants. Then, when you're ready, enter a Junior Showmanship show for dog owners ages 10 to 18. Don't expect to win at first. The more you participate, the better your—and your dog's—chances of winning.

Best in Show

Throwing a Successful
Slumber Party

The key to a great slumber party lies in the guest list. Make sure that you enjoy being with the guests and that they all get along well together. After that, the rest is a breeze. Put on popular dance music. Rent good movies. Keep food and snacks on hand. Plan a few talking games or charades. Pull out supplies and nail polish for makeovers. Arrange bedding or sleeping bags in a star shape with all heads toward the middle to make late-night conversations easier. Help your parents plan some fun for your siblings so that they won't be hanging around your party all night. Have fun!

Secret #84

Ordering Pizzas for a Slumber Party

Buy one large pizza for every three people. But ask yourself these questions before purchasing: Will you serve other foods? If so, you might want fewer pizzas. Will the rest of the family show up for a bite, or will you be up late and want a snack? Will you want pizza for breakfast? If so, you might want more pizzas. Before ordering, check to see if any of your guests are vegetarian or have allergies.

Secret #85

Training Fish to Come to You

Fish in tanks learn very quickly who feeds them. So, make sure you're the one who always feeds the fish. If you do, as soon as you walk over to the tank, the fish will swim right to you. And if you shake the food box before you feed them, they'll swim to you as soon as they hear the sound of the box. Just be sure you don't overfeed the fish. Goldfish in ponds can be trained, too. Be at the pond, with food, at the same time every day. In time, they'll even follow you around the pond waiting to be fed.

Secret #86

Sharing a Room with a Sibling

Remember that your sister needs her space, too. If she invites friends over, let her have the room. Most likely she'll do the same for you when your friends come over. Respect each other's space by defining the space. Use furniture to separate areas. Divide storage space equally. Divide dresser drawers. Share walls. Get two bulletin boards. Then decorate your area the way you want, and let your sister do the same.

Secret #87

Getting into American Girl Magazine

American Girl magazine receives thousands of letters a year from girls, and only a small handful of those girls' letters appear in the magazine. To improve your chances of being included in that handful, follow these tips from *American Girl* editors.

Make your submission unique.

If you're entering a contest or drawing a picture, try to think of something no one else will dream up. If you're writing a letter, pick out a one-of-a-kind experience from your life that will make readers say, "Wow!"

Don't leave out the details.

Explain why you're passionate about an activity, hobby, or skill. Write about a life-changing experience. The magazine uses real-life stories for "True Story," "Shining Star," and profiles. Don't forget to read the entry forms and provide all the requested information, such as your full name, address, age, and birth date.

Keep trying.

Don't quit trying to get in. Every issue offers new chances for poems, drawings, stories, photos, puzzles, and more.

americangirl.com

American Girl

Bring AG magazine to life at your **slumber party!**

4 hairstyles you'll **love**

valentines and share

Win It!
Everything
you need
to throw a
party!

Secret #88

Making a Snowman Special

Add pizzazz to your snowman this winter. Stand him on his head. Show him taking a nap. Sit him on a bench. And then decorate him with unusual things: a plant for hair or an egg-beater for a nose. Fill a spray bottle with water, add three drops of food coloring, and then spray on color. You can also turn your snowman into a giant bird feeder by pressing seed all over him. Or turn your snowman into a snowwoman, a snowchild, or a snowbear!

Secret #89

Keeping Snow Out of Your Boots

The drier you stay when out in the snow, the warmer you'll be. Slip gaiters over your boots and pant legs. These water-proof coverings keep snow out. If you don't have gaiters, cut the feet off an old pair of knee socks and slip the the sock top over the tops of your boots.

Secret #90

Making the World a Better Place

Find out where your hometown needs the most help. Talk to teachers, librarians, religious leaders, scout or 4-H leaders, school counselors, or animal shelter directors. Or pick a cause you want to support, such as childhood diabetes or breast cancer research, and contact that organization. Help out one person or one animal in need. Or get your family involved and brainstorm lots of ways to help your community: Serve food at a homeless shelter, collect coats for kids, deliver food to the elderly, clean parks and streams, help out at a vet clinic. Or plan moneymakers, such as bake sales, rummage sales, carnivals, or babysitting jobs, and donate the earnings. That's making a difference right in your own backyard.

Psst . . .

Do you have any secret instructions you'd like to share?

Write to us at:
Psst . . . Editor
American Girl
8400 Fairway Place
Middleton, WI 53562

All comments and suggestions received by American Girl may be used without compensation or acknowledgment. Sorry—photos can't be returned.

Here are some other American Girl books you might like:

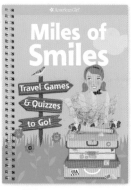

❑ I read it.

❑ I read it.

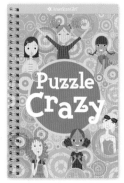

❑ I read it.

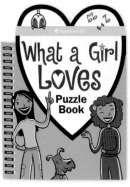

❑ I read it.

❑ I read it.

❑ I read it.

❑ I read it.